God's Grace

on a Farm Girl

CHRISTINE LAFEVER SCHNEGG

Fulton Books, Inc.
Meadville, PA

Published by Fulton Books 2021

ISBN 978-1-63860-239-2 (paperback)
ISBN 978-1-63860-240-8 (digital)

Printed in the United States of America

INTRODUCTION

Throughout my life, I have definitely had my share of struggles as well as many blessings. Much of my raising was self-taught. I have had a lot of time to think and learn from my mistakes. I feel that is one of the best ways to learn, and the learning never ends. We are all human, and we all make mistakes, but as God is our redeemer, we can pull through and strive for anything that we set our minds to.

I am not a celebrity, nor do I want fame. I feel that I have a testimony to share. The purpose of me writing this book is to let people know that they are not alone. We all have someone to turn to, no matter what the circumstances. You may have done things in your life that you're not proud of, but there's always forgiveness through Christ. I have never been a fancy person or one who keeps up with the trends. I'm just me. I am a sinner saved by grace.

CHAPTER 1

A Mother's Love

In December 1983, my life was to be forever changed. On that cold, late fall day, my dad greeted my siblings and me at our home when we arrived off the bus from school. When we heard the news, it all seemed like a bad dream. My mother, age thirty-eight, was in a car accident a short two weeks after she obtained her driver's license. She was on her way home from an appointment and was struck by an oncoming car. That Tuesday afternoon, we had learned that we lost our loving mother.

Cheryl Ann was my mother's name, and she was the greatest woman I have ever met. Being only eight years old, my recollection of her is faint, but I know in my heart she was a wonderful woman for her heart belonged to God. As big as our family was, we were all dressed and ready to go for church every Sunday morning, every Sunday night, and every Wednesday evening. My mother had a big responsibility with all of us, and being in church was her number one priority. God was quite evident in her life. Without Him, I'm not sure how she could have held up as great as she did, and most importantly, I don't know how we would have made it through her death without her showing us the way.

I am the youngest of seven siblings. The old farmhouse consisted of three bedrooms and a make-shift room in the basement that was used for a bedroom for my brothers. My parents had a total of five girls and two boys. At the time of my mother's death, my two oldest sisters were married and moved out. Not at that time, but I later come to realize how envious I was of my older siblings that they got so much more time with my mother.

My mother was the type of person that would do everything she could to help others in need although we scraped for pennies ourselves. Despite our low income, we always had a hot meal on the table for dinner and never went hungry. My parents taught us to work hard and be respectful. Every summer, it took all of us as a family working together to raise a garden. Our farm consisted of pigs, chickens, dogs, cats, and an occasional duck or two. Our uncle and aunt, from a few miles down the road, also had cattle that would graze on our farm. I will always be thankful for our country life.

I can recall very few memories of my life before I was eight. I'm not exactly sure what is normal to remember, but I hold dearly to the ones that I do. I know that we always were loved. I remember having many struggles, mostly financially, but that can be expected with so many children. My dad worked outside the home and did mostly factory or odds-and-ends jobs. My mom, worked at home, taking care of all of us. Our extended families helped when we were in desperate need which wasn't often as far as I can remember. I am so thankful to have had food in my stomach, a bed to sleep in, and a roof over my head.

There were several occasions when we would get into trouble. Just let me say that being the young-est sometimes has its advantages. I don't recall this so much, but my siblings have often told me the tales of me getting away with more than everyone else. They say all I had to do was cry and my mom would scold anyone that I blamed. Looking back, I don't think that this was quite fair, but I'm sure that I probably used this to my advantage a time or two.

I recall a memory of all of us getting in big trou-ble for playing in the road. My mom made everyone pick out a switch to be spanked with, the thicker, the better. Those little ones, as I've been told, sting worse. All my siblings took their turn at being punished, but I was not ready for mine. I ran as fast as I could to get away from my mom running after me and I even-tually got away. My mom gave up, and I received no switching! That night, it seemed as though I was also rewarded for getting away. I was the only one allowed to sit close to the television. At around six years old, my mom still let me have a bottle in the living room in the evening. I guess I was a little spoiled.

Every Christmas, my mom made it special. I can remember waking up early, creeping down the stairs, and taking a peek at the tree to see if Santa arrived. I believe that my sisters put me up to that task so that they didn't get into trouble because we weren't allowed to come down before a certain time. The tree, an artificial one, which we had for several years, was always so beautiful. It was always lit up with colorful lights, ornaments, that were mostly handmade by all of us, and strings of popcorn. I can still smell the wonderful aroma that filled the kitchen in the afternoon. The night before Sunday Christmas service, I remember my hair in rollers and sleeping an uncomfortable sleep so that it would look beautiful for church the next morning.

My mother always made memories for us. I so wish I could hug her again, especially around Christmas time. At times, I feel her angel arms embracing me. I question why God let this happen to our family but know it was for a reason. Even now, thirty-six years later, that question still arises. Now though, I am at peace with it. I have never been angry at God.

CHAPTER 2

Struggles and Coping while Growing Up

Times after my mom passed were very hard. For the next few years, I still shared the house with my two brothers, two sisters, and my dad. Somehow, we managed to make it. My dad worked, and when I wasn't in school, I was left home with my older siblings. I looked forward to going to school because, at home, my mind was not as preoccupied. The yearning to feel my mother's embrace was overwhelming. I missed her so.

My life at school was good, at least it was better than my life at home. I had a few great friends that I still have to this day. Learning was okay, and as I got older, I learned to value it more and more. My parents were old-fashioned in the way that learning home survival tactics was more important than what they were teaching in school. These days, I wish they were teaching more of the home economics that I learned when I was a child. Regardless, I decided that it was up to me to learn what I could while I was at school.

During the summer months, I would try to go down the road a couple of miles to my cousin's house to play. She was my age and had a brother a couple of years younger than us. We didn't have a telephone at that time, so I went down to my closest neighbor, which was about a mile away, to use her phone to call. I was very thankful to be able to get away from home. I enjoyed getting away from the reality of what my normal life had become.

A few years later, all but my brother, Nate, and I were left at the house. My two sisters and older brother moved out. At that time, I think I was around twelve. My dad worked the afternoon shift and I was mostly alone in the evening. Nate, sixteen, was mostly out with his friends. When he was home, he spent most of his time in the basement.

Most of my time at home was spent outside as much as I could. I was either riding my bike, walking on the road by my house, or having adventures in the woods. I also liked to play in the barn. We had a basketball court in the top loft where hay was kept. There were also some old vintage appliances in the lower part of the barn where I often played restaurant. I would imagine serving customers fresh mud pies.

I also spent a good bit of time fishing at a pond about a quarter mile from the house. There was mainly just bluegill, and they were amusing to catch as a kid. I usually used doughballs or worms that I had collected from the cow manure or from under overturned rocks. Sometimes I would go with one of my siblings and sometimes I would be alone. We always took them off our hooks and threw them back because they weren't really good for eating.

One day in the woods, I decided to go into the makeshift tree house that my older brother built. I had been in it several times, but that day was different. I climbed it by using the boards that were nailed to the tree. I was about twenty feet up, and one of the boards came off. I fell to the ground and must have hit my head on a rock. The next thing I remember was waking up on the couch in my living room with leaves in my hair. My brother, Nate, told me that he found me because I was yelling for him and then he carried me to the house.

In the wintertime, I filled my afternoons and evenings listening to the radio in my room or watching movies. I also liked going through my clothes, which were mostly hand-me-downs, to see what I could wear to school the next day. I also had normal homework and studying. My life wasn't very exciting at that time and mostly spent alone.

Sharing my memories of my childhood, my life seemed pretty normal. Although, as I think back, there are a lot of blurred images of what my past was. There were a lot of times when I wish that I could blot out the memories. The struggles that I had as a child growing up without my mother has affected me my entire life. I have dealt with all my emotional stress on my own with the power of prayer. I have learned to cope. I believe that I am strong because of what my mom had taught me. I learned from her the truth of how real God is.

CHAPTER 3

My Best Friend

I was in the second grade when my mother passed away, and that year, there was a girl in my class that I was so thankful for. She was my best friend. Her name is Melissa, and she also rode my bus. My cousin that lived down the road from me, I was very close with, but that year, she was placed in a different class. I can remember that Melissa and I were inseparable that year. That was the year that a lot of change happened in my life. Melissa, at that time I didn't realize, was exactly what I needed.

Melissa and I, over the years, have made so many memories. In third grade, we were placed in different classes. Her cousin lived close by and also rode our bus. That year, we were riding the bus home from school, and something very surprising happened! For the first and only time in my life, I got into a fight. My cousin, a neighbor girl, and I were sitting in one seat and Melissa and her cousin sat behind us that day. Melissa's cousin accused my cousin of stealing chalk, and that's how it began. The whole bus was cheering the fight on. Even the bus driver participated in the cheering. In the end, no one was hurt, really. I ended up giving Melissa a bloody lip, and I had a piece of gum stuck in my hair. I got the raw end of the deal, in my opinion, but it was definitely an experience I will never forget.

After third grade, Melissa and I were best friends again. We tried to spend as much of our free time together. Sleepovers happened often but not as often as we would have liked. Melissa's parents were my adopted mom and dad, or so I felt. In the years to come, that became more relevant. I, as a child and young adult, did not want to be home. Being with my friend was an escape from my reality.

I have so many memories with my dear friend. When it was warm outside, we spent most of our time on adventures. Melissa and I went on several hikes in the woods, played in the creek, went fishing, or whatever we could to be away. Melissa's little sister was often with us, not that we necessarily wanted that, but that's the way it was. We were often not very nice to her. We teased her and played a few tricks here and there. There were times though that we would let her play along. One time, we had strung an old cassette tape around the house. We would maneuver ourselves through the tape, and if we touched it, we would have to go back to the start. Melissa's little sister, being smaller than us, seemed to have an easier time and would often win. We also spent a lot of time talking, making up stories, and playing Nintendo.

Melissa and I also liked to go over to her Grandpa's house, which was right next door. We often climbed an old tree in the backyard and pretended that the leaves were money.

Another memorable pastime for us was taking pictures of each other. Melissa and I would gather up clothes that we wanted to change into for our photo shoots and head out to the woods. One time, we finished up with our session and then realized that the film in the camera wasn't working properly and that the photo shoot was a waste, but we still had a lot of fun. We also had a few photo shoots in our houses. I wish that I had a photo album of just our old pictures. What a wonderful reminder of our friendship.

Melissa and I went on quite a few camping adventures. Most of the time, it was in the field across from my house or a few miles down the road on my uncle's property. One night, in the field across my house, we were telling scary stories. Then I remember playing a song with the CD player that said something about Chucky from *Child's Play*. We were pretty scared, then my dog started barking outside the tent! It took us a while to fall asleep that night, and when we awoke in the morning, we found a set of deer antlers! On my uncle's property, there was a pond where we often went swimming and fishing. On one side of the pond, there was a flat spot where we put our tent. Melissa and I would take our favorite snacks with us, mostly junk food, along with a radio, fishing poles, and other essentials for the night. Talking and telling stories was the best part of it all.

As Melissa and I grew into older teenagers, we were still close friends, but our minds got preoccupied with other things (boys and other friends), and we drifted apart somewhat. After graduation, we drifted a little more, but after thirty-eight years, Melissa is still my true best friend. She is the type of girl (well, woman now) that I can trust with anything. She is also the best advice giver. Melissa was a great deal of my past, and I am so very thankful to have such a wonderful friend.

CHAPTER 4

My Brother Nate

After my mom passed, it was so hard on all of us. My brother, Nate, and I were very traumatized because we were so young. I was only eight, and Nate was twelve. We didn't spend that much time together. I guess because we had different interests and friends. Over the course of the few years following our mother's death, we grew apart even more.

After Nate got his driver's license and a car, I hardly ever saw him. I was home alone a lot at that time. When Nate did come home, most of the time, he was high on drugs. We would get into a lot of heated arguments but can't really remember what they were about. Nate struggled with fitting in although he had a caring personality. He got into the wrong crowd and made some bad decisions.

Nate would often scare me when he would come home. I didn't know how to handle someone that was addicted to drugs. I tried to just stay in my room most of the time. One morning, I woke up, and Nate had absolutely no hair on him. His head was bald, and his legs and arms were shaved completely smooth. Nate had said that someone broke into our house and did it while he was sleeping. I believed that he was high on something and did it himself.

One of the scariest moments of my life was when Nate had a confrontation with someone that lived close by. Nate and I were home alone after school, and it was still daylight. The people that Nate had wronged came to the house and knocked on the door. We were both terrified of what they might do, so we hid in the bathroom and kept very quiet. The people outside were trying to break in! I was so scared! After about ten minutes, or eternity, so it felt, they left. Nate and I both came outside to see if they had damaged anything, and my heart sank. There on the porch was one of our beloved farm cats lying dead on the porch. There was a lump in the pit of my stomach for a long time after that.

Three months before Nate was to graduate high school, he dropped out. No one really knew why other than his problems with addiction. He was on the run after that. I would see him occasionally when he needed money or food, but most of the time, he would crash at a friends' house or in his car. He was forced to go to rehab after getting in trouble with the law, but he got out and went right down the same broken path.

The last time that I saw Nate was the summer that I was sixteen. He didn't want to come to the house because he didn't want to face our dad, so I met him on a nearby gravel road. He wanted some money, so I gave him all I had, which wasn't much. I didn't know that was the last time I would see him. I remember that we parted on good terms and said goodbye. Thinking back, I'm not sure if I told him that I loved him, but I'm sure he knew.

Nate went down to Florida to escape his troubles. He found a job and was working and do all right as far as we knew. Three years later, he was on a business trip in Alabama. They found his body in a hotel room. The autopsy showed that the cause of death was a cocaine overdose. It took a few weeks to contact the family because he had no identification on him. The only trace to his life in Ohio was a telephone number of a close friend in his wallet. When we finally got the news, my dad went to Alabama to identify the body.

Addiction is a terrible thing. It makes you do and say things that are out of your context as a person. Nate was such a kind and loving person, but he hurt the people he loved many times, including me. Most of it was by lying, but he often stole things to sell to support his addiction. Nate stole off of neighbors, friends, and family. My dear sweet brother Nathaniel left this world way too early. At age twenty-four, he had been through so much mostly because of bad decisions that he made. Nate was so funny and had a heart of gold. Despite the hard times, he also made me laugh. He was my brother, and I loved him so.

We all have choices in our lives. Unfortunately for a lot of children, there are hard decisions to make at a young age. As humans, we can learn from our mistakes and the mistakes of the people that are close to us but not always. My brother Nate and I both came from the same home and chose two separate paths. I am not saying that I am saintlike. Believe me, I have had my share of mistakes, but when it comes down to it, the bottom line is, that it is our own choice to be who we are.

CHAPTER 5

High School Years

In high school, I considered myself a congenial person. I avoided those who wanted to fight and bully me and talked to everyone. I tried to get decent grades and go to school every day. My homelife was a little different. My dad remarried when I was fourteen, and I was thankful. My stepmom treated me like one of her own, and I appreciated her very much for that. Nate left shortly after Dad remarried, so it was just me living at home.

My older sisters would let me stay with them from time to time, on weekends and during the summer. I enjoyed a change of scenery. They mentored me as a young teen and all tried to spend time with me. They all knew it was hard on me growing up without Mom. I so wished I had her with me, but my sisters helped with the pain.

When I started dating, although, I didn't ask my sisters any questions. The only thing I really knew about sex was what they taught in school. When my mom took us took church, they didn't teach us much about refraining from intimacy until we were married because I was so young when she passed. After that, my churchgoing was almost nonexistent. So there I was, a teenager that was developed before most of the other girls and had no clue what a healthy relationship was supposed to be like.

When I was in junior high, the boys started noticing me and giving me attention. It was something that I wasn't used to, and it felt good to be wanted. I had many voids in my life and felt alone quite a bit. I had many different boyfriends, but it all seemed to be more of a joke to everyone to see how many relationships I could have. The boys that I didn't have as a boyfriend would tease me and call me names. I was all right with that because at least I was getting attention.

The summer between junior high and high school was when I lost my virginity. It was to someone that didn't care about me. The relationship only lasted a few weeks, and then it was over. I then met a boy that was very good to me. I dated him for almost two years. He went to a different school, so I didn't see him through the week. My dad and stepmom would take me to see him on Sundays. Although it was hard to slip away at times from his parents, we always found time to be alone. He will always hold a piece of my heart.

I ended that relationship, which was one of the hardest things I had done up until that point. I was sixteen and got my license. Instead of wanting to settle down so young, I had other desires. My friends and I would drive around a local town. The attention from boys continued, and I continued to enjoy it. I got my first job that summer and got to know different people than the ones that I grew up with in school. Over the next few years, I made a lot of bad decisions. I had many relationships and many hardships.

I met quite a few new friends and had a lot of great memories. I pretty much did what I wanted. My dad and stepmom both worked, and I took full advantage of that. My dad never really asked too many questions. I would just tell him that I was staying with a friend and then just stay out as late as I wanted or come back the next morning. I guess you could say that I had a college partying life in high school.

When I turned eighteen, I started going to bars. I loved to be around friends, dancing and playing pool. I went to many parties with a slightly older crowd. I looked forward to the weekends when I could be with my partying friends. I fit in with them and felt comfortable. Although, deep in my heart, I felt that this kind of life wasn't right.

I so wish I could go back and change those days. You see, as much as I loved it then, I found myself thinking back, I was lucky to be alive. There are so many things that could have went wrong. Another disadvantage to this kind of life is that I had no respect for myself, and in turn, others had no respect for me. This put a hole in the pit of my stomach.

Only I could change it. I needed help but felt like I had no one to turn to. I had friends and family, but the embarrassment of my wrongdoings kept my feelings bottled up inside me.

CHAPTER 6

My First Marriage

Through my rough teenage years, I met a man after graduation. He was very kind and had a wonderful heart. I met him in a local bar that I hung out with my friends. He worked there as the bouncer. This man had a smile that could melt your heart, and he definitely did mine. We had our first date and went back to his place. That was the night that we fell in love. I stayed the night and never went back to my home on the farm.

We lived together for about a year and then we married. I was nineteen years old and my new husband was ten years older than me. He was married once before and already had two children. I wanted one of my own, but my husband didn't. I know that this issue should have been better addressed and confirmed before we said I do, but it wasn't. So there I was, married with no future of having a family of my own.

My husband and I had a few other differences, and we both made mistakes, mostly me. I wanted out of this new marriage. The guilt inside me was unbearable. I can't remember what my parents were like before my mom passed away other than a few arguments that they had. I had been through so much in my life already, but I take full responsibility for my actions.

My first marriage only lasted two and a half years. I was mostly at fault, and there are no good reasons for my mistakes. My husband was overall a good man and didn't deserve what I put him through. We signed papers for dissolution, and our marriage was over.

Over the years after our divorce, I still battled with the guilt. I still cared for him but knew that I could never go back. About ten years had passed and I finally got up the nerve and arranged for us to meet. I was with one of my sisters and my brother and he was with a close friend of his. We all met in a local tavern. That night, I apologized for everything that I had done wrong.

After that, a weight was lifted. I was able to apologize, and he accepted it and was very kind. A few months later, I got the news that he passed away. I just couldn't believe it. An important part of my past was gone, and I am so glad that I was able to talk with him to try to explain and make amends. I believe God gave me that opportunity, and I was blessed by it.

I was young, grew up in a broken home, and was taken advantage of at a young age by people that I trusted. Looking back, I so wished that I had a professional person to talk to about my life. From a young age, I wanted to write a book. I guess it was a way of crying out. I kept everything bottled up though other than telling my best friend. Regardless of my childhood, I have tried to own up to my mistakes. I guess that is part of growing up.

CHAPTER 7

Kevin

Today I woke up thinking of Kevin, which I often do, and thought it was time to introduce him. I had a dream about him again. Every dream is fairly the same. Most of the time, we are back in the trailer where we lived before we built the new house. The trailer was pretty rundown. Some of the electrical didn't work, which was a little scary. The carpet in the master bedroom was growing mushrooms because of an unknown water leak from the hot water tank. It served its purpose, though. Kevin and I spent thirteen years in that trailer before moving into the new house. Our children were brought home there. I often miss it or, more so, its memories.

Kevin and I met when I was sixteen, and he was eighteen. I was a cashier for the summer at a local grocery store, and he was a bagger. I lived locally but went to a different school. There were several people that worked there that I will never forget. Kevin was dating someone else at that time, so we didn't really hang out until that fall when his relationship temporarily dissolved. Being a teenager at the time and just getting my license in February that year, I wasn't ready to settle into a long-term relationship. So at the end of that year, I parted ways from Kevin until years later.

The next time that I ran into Kevin was at a high school football game. I was walking around the end zone to use the restroom, and he turned, and I saw him. I immediately went to him, and we spoke for a few minutes. It was a normal conversation to catch up on what we had been doing the last few years. Our conversation ended with me giving him my phone number. I was very surprised to hear from him the next day. Kevin called and asked if I would like to be his date at his cousin's wedding that day. Of course, I said yes, and he picked me up a few hours later.

From the moment I got into his truck, there were lots to catch up on. We both were nervous but mostly excited to see each other again. It took us a little over an hour to drive to the wedding, so we had some time to talk. His cousin's wedding was beautiful, but we were both anxious to get back to our conversation. In between the wedding and reception, we took a little ride so we could have a few minutes alone. Kevin pulled over on the side of the road so that we could have a more intimate talk. At that moment, Kevin and I looked at each other, and we shared a kiss. I thought my heart was going to explode. We returned to the reception shortly after, and I caught the bouquet. For the next few months, we were inseparable.

It was September when we started dating, and by December, Kevin had asked me to marry him. Kevin lived with his parents at that time, and we looked at a piece of property that would possibly be our home. We planned for an October wedding the next year. Although, the next month, in January, I got really nervous. I had just gotten out of marriage the year before, and I suddenly felt like I was moving way too fast. The next ten months, Kevin and I spent separated.

I missed Kevin so much but knew that I had to set my mind straight before I could have a long, committed relationship. I even took a trip to visit a friend in California for a few months. Kevin and I hadn't talked the whole time we were separated, so I didn't even know where he was or what he was doing at that time. I had a lot of time to think, and the rocky beaches of the Pacific Ocean were just what I needed. I realized that I was ready. I realized that Kevin was the one that I wanted to spend the rest of my life with.

For the next few months, I lived with Melissa's sister in her grandpa's old house. Kevin was cautious about letting me back into his life, so we just took it slow. By February that next year, he was ready to let me back into his life. During our separation, Kevin had bought the property that we had once looked at and moved a trailer there that he had purchased from one of his friends. I moved my things from Melissa's sister's place that month. The next few months, even though wonderful, I was proving that I was there to stay. Then tragedy arose.

At that time, I was working as a waitress at a restaurant. I was a corporate trainer and was training a new opening store. The training lasted a week, so I and the other trainers stayed in a hotel. One morning that week, I awoke to a phone call. Kevin's brother's wife, at that time, was on the line. After I was alert enough to understand what she was saying, my heart immediately was in shock. I had learned that Kevin was in a car accident and was in the hospital with a broken neck and several other injuries. I gathered my things and went to him. It took me about five hours to get to him, but I finally arrived. Kevin had fallen asleep at the wheel and had crashed into a tree. I stayed with him and a few days later brought him home.

For the next several months, I took care of him. My heart ached to think how much pain he must have been in. Kevin suffered from his neck being broken in two places, a couple of cracked ribs, and a sprained ankle, among many other minor injuries. I went back to work the next week, and a few months later, I got a second job as a cashier to help cover some of the bills. Eventually, Kevin went back to work, and everything was good again.

In 2002, I started a new job as a manager in a local fast-food place that was opening, and in March 2003, Kevin and I finally got married. It was a beautiful wedding and was all done in a hunting theme. Kevin was an avid hunter, so camo and turkey calls were just up his alley. My matron of honor was of course Melissa, and she helped me make all the bridesmaids' dresses and the vests for the men, all camouflage. It was a wonderful day to celebrate with family and friends.

In May 2007, we were blessed with a beautiful baby boy, and we named him after my brother and a very dear friend of Kevin's that both passed away. It took us four years of trying to conceive to get our wonderful blessing. Kevin and I had a miscarriage in the early stages of pregnancy a year before, and it was so very heartbreaking because we wanted children so. We experienced another miscarriage a few years after our son was born, but in December 2011, we were blessed with a perfect baby girl. Our family was complete.

The building of our new house, which was right beside the trailer, was very exciting. In the spring of 2012 is when we broke ground. Kevin and I, along with his dad and a few Amish builders, completed by November that year, and we moved in. We celebrated our daughter's first birthday and Christmas in our new house, and it all seemed like a dream come true. We finally had everything we wanted, and then disaster struck our little family.

CHAPTER 8

Kevin Part 2

On January 9, 2013, my life once again came to a halt. Kevin was driving to work the midnight shift at a local coal mine. It was a cold night. As he was driving, he hit a patch of black ice and veered to the opposite side of the road where he was struck by two oncoming cars. Kevin lost his life that night.

I woke up at five thirty that morning and couldn't go back to sleep. I then heard someone pulling into the driveway, so I went downstairs to see who it was. Kevin's parents, along with a highway state patrol, were at my door. I let them in, and the officer explained what had happened. Shortly before midnight, Kevin died. The state patrol went to Kevin's parents first and then came to me. I was in such shock and couldn't believe it at first.

Kevin's parents stayed the day, and more and more family and friends came to comfort me and the kids. Everyone was so wonderful to me, and I appreciate everything so much. I had a houseful for several days and was very thankful. The little town that we lived outside of was also very wonderful. I was truly blessed with so much love and support.

The planning of my husband's funeral was not what I thought that I would be doing at such a young age. I was only thirty-seven with two young children. Kevin's parents and I made the arrangements together and tried to do what Kevin would have wanted. We had the viewing on Kevin's birthday and put him to rest the next day.

I cannot explain the pain that I suffered. I had lost the love of my life and the father of my children. My son was five, and my daughter had just turned one the month before. We had only been living in the new house for two months before the tragedy. Kevin and I had many great years together. I wish that there would have been a lot more.

I feel so sorrowful for my children that they never really had the chance to know their dad. I knew how it felt to lose a parent at a young age. I was worried that I could not do it by myself. I always have wanted the best for them. My children have completely changed my life. I went so many years wondering if it was even possible to conceive and deliver them. I could not imagine my life without them.

The years to come after the death of my husband were the hardest thing I have ever gone through. I could not have made it without God. There is no way that I could have even imagined living without having such a wonderful provider. I have been blessed with so many things in my life. All of it is owed to Him.

Kevin always said that he believed in God but never wanted to talk about his faith. He was afraid to die. I think the biggest part of him being afraid was that he would be leaving behind his loved ones. He was the same age as my mom was when she passed. I'm not sure if that was a coincidence or if it happened that way for a reason. I often question things about life but know that God has a plan.

Several things happened prior to Kevin's death that led his family and I to believe that God was preparing us for what was about to happen. Kevin always wanted to make sure that I knew how to drive the mower, what bills we had, and where the paper for our life insurance was. He also talked about his funeral arrangements, which I disregarded because I thought that we were going to grow old together. Kevin also wanted to make sure we had lots of pictures and videos of us as a family. The kids and I will cherish those forever. Kevin also made comments to his family that made us look back and think. One day, he taught one of his nephews how to tickle his mom (Kevin's sister). Kevin told him that he needed to take over after he was gone.

There are several things that happened after Kevin's passing that have made me feel that he is here in spirit with us. The morning that we found out the news, the kids were still sleeping, and Kevin's parents and I were in the dining room, trying to fathom our recent news. The baby monitor was on in my daughter's room, and all of a sudden, we hear her say "Dada." Coincidence? I believe she saw her daddy whether it was a dream or while she was awake. Either way, I knew.

Kevin was an avid hunter. He loved the thrill of it as well as the purpose of feeding his family. After he passed, I did some landscaping in front of the house in memory of him. One morning, I went outside in the spring, and there were turkey feathers in the landscaping! The wind must have brought them in with a little help from Kevin. Another time, I found a deer antler there. I really can't explain that one other than Kevin made it so.

My son had a dream one night about his dad that confirmed again that Kevin was watching over us. He dreamed that his dad came to him in his room with angel wings and gave him a hug. Kevin told him in that powerful dream that everything was going to be all right. I, too, often have dreams about Kevin, just letting me know that his presence is still around us. I am extremely thankful for that.

CHAPTER 9

Kevin's Angel

There are things that happen in this life that are unexplainable. There are also people in this world that touch our lives in a way that changes us. I have had several people touch my life that who has made me who I am—my mom, my best friend, my pastor, my husband, my kids, etc. There are so many wonderful people in this world. Sometimes if we are lucky, we meet people that in one instance can turn our world around and bring new meaning to what we value most.

Kevin had a life-altering experience just a few short months before he passed away. It was in an ordinary place where you wouldn't expect to be moved in such a way. It was late November, and we were getting settled into our new home. Kevin had to take his truck to have maintenance done at a local dealership. The wait took a few hours, so it was natural to make small talk with the other customers waiting to be serviced. That day, Kevin met someone that he didn't expect. A person that changed his life.

Kevin was among several other customers that day who would come and go. A conversation started between him and one lady who was there for a large portion of his visit. Kevin described her as this perfect lady. She was well-dressed with her handbag setting in her lap. She was a retired schoolteacher that moved to the area from a different state. Kevin felt unusually comfortable around this lady. As the conversation progressed, she seemed to pull personal things out of him. She would ask him questions, and he would willfully respond.

Kevin talked about his life and his family. He told this lady about his children, his new house, and his life as a coal miner. They spent hours talking. He even shared some of his hardships and struggles. She was very interested in knowing him. Kevin needed her that day for what happened next changed his life.

The service agent came and called her name. The lady got up and paid for her service, and she was ready to go. Before she left, she came back to Kevin and wanted to say goodbye. She asked Kevin for a hug, so he stood up. That lady looked at him in the eyes, put her hands on his cheeks, and said, "Prepare to feel the arms of God around you." She gave him a hug and left.

Kevin's truck was ready, and he went to the service department window to settle his bill. The person at the window gave Kevin his total, and something didn't seem right. It was considerably lower than expected. That lady that he spent hours talking to paid for a portion of his bill! He was in disbelief and was very grateful to this stranger, this wonderful woman. She not only moved him in a spiritual way that day but also had the most wonderful, giving heart.

Kevin came home, and he was so excited about this new spiritual motivation. The motivation of the Holy Spirit that this one lady, this angel, had shown Kevin that day. Kevin had to tell everyone he was close to about her. After that day, Kevin was different. He seemed not to be worried about the little things. He was very calm and enjoyed life more. For the first time in a long time, we were beyond happy. Our little family was in a safe home, the bills were paid, and most importantly, Kevin's heart was right with God.

This lady had led Kevin closer to Christ that day. I believe that 100 percent. Kevin always believed in God, but he never wanted to talk about Christianity. He was different after that day. Other than being more open about his faith, I could see many changes. He was happier and didn't worry about the little things anymore.

After Kevin's passing, I was determined to find the lady that changed his life. I called the dealership where they met and the person that I spoke with had heard about Kevin's passing and also knew exactly who the lady was that he talked to that day. I then gave them my phone number and asked them to contact her to give her my information. This lady, Kevin's angel, called me a few days after. I heard her sweet voice and knew that she was an angel. We talked for a little while that day and shared her interpretation of her and Kevin's conversation. She thought the world of Kevin and was so devastated by the news of his passing. She was so heartbroken for me and his children.

Kevin's angel and I have talked over the years and kept in contact. I have been so blessed by her being in our lives. She truly is a wonderful, God-loving woman. I will never forget her and always hold her close to my heart. My kids have enjoyed her so much. Someday they will realize what she truly did for their dad and how blessed that he was to meet her.

CHAPTER 10

Life After

I have truly been blessed with so many wonderful things in my life. My faith and my children are the most important to me. God has helped me my whole life, even when I wasn't as close to Him as I should have been. In my darkest days, I felt His comfort and knew that He was there.

The days after Kevin's passing have been the hardest times of my life thus far. I know that Kevin is at rest and that he isn't suffering through unbearable migraines anymore. Though missing him is the most heart-wrenching feeling. Some say that time heals all wounds. If you are talking about physical wounds, then yes, this is true. Emotional wounds never heal. I am truly as brokenhearted as I was eight years ago. My heart aches for me and my children.

I believe that there is a reason for everything that happens to us. I believe that God strengthens us through our trials. We all have struggles and sadness in our lives. How we respond to those struggles make us who we are. Some of us turn to drugs to ease our pain. Some of us turn to lustful desires to get our minds off what is bothering us. Some of us put ourselves into a pit of deep depression and feel so alone. We feel that life isn't worth living anymore. I am telling you as a witness, there is another way.

Ever since I was a teen, I wanted to share my story. Back then, I was going through so much turmoil that I felt led to write. I did start a few times but never gave it everything I had. That seems like forever ago, and I have been through so much more. I have also received many more blessings. My purpose in writing about my life is in hopes that I help someone. If one person reads this and realizes that they are not alone, then my heart is happy.

I am a Christian, and I am not afraid to admit that. I know that more people than not in this world don't believe that there is a God. It is my choice as a person and an American to believe the way that I do. It has saved my life many times. God fills my life with joy and love. That is truly our purpose here on earth. Our purpose is to love, help others, be humble, and be kind.

I came to a new realization within the last few months and wanted to share this also. When I am mowing the grass is when I do most of my deep thinking and often find myself in tears. I often ask God why certain things have happened. I know that there are reasons but I just need to trust God that He will take care of me, and He definitely has. I came to a point one day while on the mower and just asked myself, "Why am I crying? I am so blessed! Why am I feeling so sorry for myself" I quickly said, like I often do, "Snap out of it, LaFever!" LaFever is my maiden name and what I call myself when I need to straighten up. It is human to feel sorry for ourselves, but I speak to you from experience. Don't let it bring you down! We all deserve better than how we value our own life. God values us so much more than we ever will. Why can't we do the same?

If we, as human beings, are suffering, it is our choice to either give in to the evil that tears us down or to turn things around to make us right. It is our choice to take the next right step in a positive direction. We all have that choice. My advice is, don't let evil win. Be honest and be kind. We are all blessed with life on this beautiful planet. Live life in love.

ABOUT THE AUTHOR

Christine LaFever Schnegg lives in the hills of the Ohio Valley. She has two loving children, a seven-year-old black Lab, and four rambunctious felines. God's Grace on a Farm Girl is her first and only publishing.

Before writing her biography, Christine has always dreamed of sharing her story. She hopes that her experiences will reach someone that is struggling and help them in some way. Growing up on a farm with a big family is both rewarding and challenging. God only gives us what we can handle.

Christine has been a stay-at-home mom and seamstress for over fifteen years. She sees herself as strong-willed as well as independent. Christine tries to be crafty as well as handy and is not afraid to get her hands dirty. She loves the country's peacefulness.

CPSIA information can be obtained
at www.ICGtesting.com
Printed in the USA
LVHW111334220722
724050LV00002B/192

9 781638 602392